To June -
(+ maybe Fred)
thanks for stopping -
we enjoy a little brouha
occasionally -

Love Marlite
& Darel
March 87

Remarkable Words
with
Astonishing Origins

Bistro

Remarkable Words

with

Astonishing Origins

by
John Train

Illustrations by Pierre Le-Tan
Foreword by Alan Pryce-Jones

Clarkson N. Potter, Inc. | Publishers, New York
Distributed by Crown Publishers, Inc.

Inquiries should be addressed to Clarkson N. Potter, Inc., One Park
Avenue, New York, New York 10016

Printed in the United States of America
Published simultaneously in Canada by General Publishing Company Limited

Library of Congress Cataloging in Publication Data

Train, John.
   Remarkable words with astonishing origins.

   Includes index.
    1. English language—Etymology.   I.   Title.
PE1574.T77 1980   422   80-15831
ISBN: 0-517-541858

10 9 8 7 6 5 4 3 2 1

First Edition

Designed by Katy Homans
Type set in Monotype Dante by Michael & Winifred Bixler

CONTENTS

Flirt

FOREWORD

John Train is a man of many facets. One depicts a serious New York investment counselor. Another shows the compiler of three extremely funny books, Remarkable Names, Even More Remarkable Names, *and* Remarkable Occurrences: *each of which, in successive years, alleviated the pangs of Christmas gift-giving for a grateful public.*

Now he turns a third face toward us: that of a painstaking etymologist, who is yet not so serious as all that. Etymology is, he knows, an austere subject, but in spite of new responsibilities, cheerfulness keeps breaking through. The reader enlarges, so to speak, his laugh, as he switches from consideration, three years ago, of the Reverend Canaan Banana, of Rhodesia; then, the following year, to the state of Ohio, where in 1895 there were only two cars, of which he notes dryly "They collided"; and finally today to the Chinese origin of the word ketchup.

What is common to all these compilations is a passion for surprises and a deadpan talent for conveying that passion. I have little doubt that this idiosyncrasy pursues the author even into investment counseling. In fact, I understand that it's precisely the unexpected but true that creates investment opportunity, and that Mr. Train is a master at discovering it.

John Train has already unearthed British plumbers named Plummer and Leek, and Mr. Vroom, the South African motorcycle dealer. And we have learned that Beau Brummell kept a special man to make only the thumbs of his gloves. If oddness creeps about the world—or anyway Mr. Train's world—with the obduracy of pachysandra in a shady border, it is possible to view future volumes with apprehension.

But also with delight. These four short books may seem easy to confect. But in reality they display a deftness of touch and a consistent fantasy which saves them from that enemy of the humorist, whimsy. They also give comfort by assuring the rest of us that a world which must

7

usually appear workaday and totally dedicated to prose still contains areas of wild poetry to explore.

Mr. Train has made each of these areas very much his own, and he has also found just the right illustrator in Pierre Le-Tan. The question for the readers, on turning the last page, must be, what next? What next?

ALAN PRYCE-JONES

PREFACE

Language is the highest form of culture, and surely word origins are the most fascinating element of language. It is extraordinary to think that the terms we use every day run right back to the dawn of man, and in working their way down to us through the millennia have been scarred and altered by all the accidents of history and geography through which they have passed.

Words dwell in our minds like insects in a forest, or, indeed, like the countless friendly organisms that inhabit the human body. We could scarcely exist without them. They illustrate what one might call cultural Darwinism. New words arrive—borne by conquest, commerce, or science—and supplant their predecessors. But the old words never fade entirely away. They linger faintly in the shadows, understudies hoping to be called back on stage. That is why the English language is incomparably richer in nuances than its rivals, although, since always in flux, it is less precise. Because of this, English offers an unusual challenge. There is more to understand: more words, evolving senses of those words, multiple cultural backgrounds.

People unaware of the origins of the words they use don't quite realize what they are saying. They are precluded from the mot juste. Take the word dilapidated. *Coming from Latin* lapis, *"stone," it refers to crumbling masonry. So to talk about a dilapidated overcoat, for instance, may convey interesting suggestions of falling masonry (or buttons), but is obviously weaker than to speak of a threadbare overcoat, just as speaking of a threadbare wall would be silly. I am always exasperated by references to a* library of wine *in gushy magazine articles.* Liber *means "book," after all.*

The search for word origins is complicated by interesting traps. For instance, in earlier centuries devising conjectural etymologies out of whole cloth was considered to be a legitimate activity. So Anglo-Saxon terms were blithely given fantastic Greek and Latin sources that could never have been. Only the more systematic etymology of recent generations has rooted out many of these whimsies.

The reader is warned against plausible explanations of common words on the basis of single episodes. These tales are usually wrong: e.g., accounting for pumpernickel as Napoleon's observation that it was "bon pour Nickel," his horse,* or the sirloin canard, for which see page 49, or the notion that marmalade† was offered as a cure to Mary Queen of Scots, Marie Malade.

Folk-etymology is a mine field. Take the English country term for asparagus. Finding the name peculiar, the country folk transformed it into sparrowgrass, which seemed more sensible. The Far Eastern English word compound, in the sense of a large enclosure, was originally Malay kampong. There are a number of other examples in the text, such as hobson-jobson and humble pie.

Back-formation, of which an example is described under Cambridge, is similar.

Another curious category is ghost words, which arise from the inaccuracies of dictionary-makers. A list of them is found at the end of the Oxford English Dictionary. As an example the reader might consider the evolution, over five centuries, of a business of ferrets into a freamyng, described on page 54. Sometimes authors, misunderstanding older texts, invent false senses for words. Sir Walter Scott was a specialist, derring-do being an example. He found the word in Spenser, who, however, had got it incorrectly from Lidgate, who had in turn garbled a text of Chaucer.

Then, there is the vast field of disputed origins. Often, as with archaeology or paleontology, one is reconstructing history on the basis of fragments, which lend themselves to different interpretations. For example, while the standard sources agree that mumbo jumbo (see page 59) comes from the Mandingo language, some authorities aver that

* In fact it comes from German pumpern, "fart."

† From Portuguese marmelada, "quince."

it means "*a witch doctor with a feather headdress*," while others, equally learned, hold for "*Be off, troublesome grandmother!*" One often gets the desperate feeling that there are no absolutely certain etymologies.

Welsh rarebit, originally the same cheese dish but called Welsh rabbit, typifies the category of genteelisms. It was a modest joke, suggesting that the Welsh were so poor they ate cheese and called it rabbit. But pompous menu writers couldn't accept anything that modest, and so came up with the baseless theory of the rarebit.

An aspect of language that "moderns" often don't recognize is that "primitive" people frequently have much larger and richer vocabularies than ours, and understand them better. Indeed, literacy may, like television, enfeeble language, not enhance it. Homer didn't read or write. Traveling in the Middle East I have heard Arab intellectuals say, "I must go and live among the Bedouins for a while and learn to speak Arabic again." Bedouin Arabic is more generously studded with proverbial wisdom than the language of the city dwellers, corrupted by advertising lingo and the debased usage of the media. I suspect that if my grandfather, who died a century ago, returned to Earth, the three things that would surprise him most would be telecommunications, inflation, and the drastic shrinkage of our vocabulary. The rest was largely foreseen by Jules Verne.

Certainly, those who aren't conscious of the sources of their language, like those who subsist on canned vegetables, miss a lot: the tang and aroma are gone. I hope this little book will contribute to enlivening language for the reader. As Auden said, through etymology words become brief lyrics about themselves.

—J. T.

Berserk

DISORDERS

Amuck

When a Malay runs *amok* he seizes his *kris* and dashes forth to hack at anyone he encounters. It is said that to get in the mood he sometimes first binds his testicles with agonizing tightness (cf. *Berserk*).

Bedlam

A contraction* of *Bethlehem* from the Hospital of St. Mary of Bethlehem, a London lunatic asylum.

Bethlehem is the Hebrew *Beth-lehem*, "House of bread."

Berserk

Literally, "bear shirt."

The Norse sagas describe a family who went into battle in a frenzy of blood lust, clad only in bearskins; by extension all furious fighters were called "Berserkers." Similarly, some Celts, when in a fighting rage, took off their clothes and attacked the enemy naked.

Brouhaha

From the Hebrew *barook habbah*, "blessed-the-comer"; as in "Blessed be he who cometh in the name of the Lord."

---

* *Like the shrinkage of Mary* Magdalen *into* maudlin.

LOVE

Boudoir

From the French *bouder*, "pout." So a *boudoir* is a room
where madame can go and sulk.* A lady can also do so in
her *sulky*: a carriage for one.

Bridal

A *bridal* party is expected to drink a lot. The word comes
from the Old English "bride-ale" that was drunk at mar-
riages before champagne became the rule.

A *buxom* bride should love, honor, and above all obey,
since the word originally meant "pliant" or "obedient."

Her consort was formerly the *goom* or "man." He was
later (and somewhat insultingly) reduced to a mere sta-
bleboy—*groom*—by folk-etymology.

---

* *And where she might say to herself,* "Je m'en fous comme de l'an quar-
ante." *The French use this strange phrase, which means literally "I don't
care any more about it than for the year 40," in the sense of "I couldn't care
less."*

It apparently survives from a Crusader's expression, Je m'en fous comme de l'al-Koran, *"I don't care any more about it than for the Koran."*

14

Boudoir

Bugger

The Cathari, a Bulgarian heretical sect of the Middle Ages, believed in eliminating sin by letting humanity die out through abstention from sex.

They were, inevitably, reproached for sodomy. Persons of that tendency came to be called "Bulgars": Latin *Bulgarus*, French *bougre*, English *bugger*.

Catamite

The passive partner among two male homosexuals. The word has evolved over countless centuries from *Ganymede* (son of King Tros of Troy), whom Zeus carried off to be his cupbearer and sex object, and whom the Romans called *Catamitus*.

Flirt

Flirt started out from Italy long ago referring to flowers, and reappeared there from England as a romantic euphemism.

Italian picture magazines like to print breathless accounts of the latest Riviera playboy *"passando un idillio con la sua ultimissima flirt,"** pronounced "fleert." They consider this delicate expression for "mistress" quite English, but in fact it comes from the French *fleureter*, and ulti-

* *"Making out with a groovy chick."*

mately from Italian *fiorare*, to "throw bouquets" of compliments.

The idea is echoed in the Spanish expression for making flattering comments to a passing girl: *echar flores*, to "throw flowers."

Miniature

The miniature of her loved one in a lady's locket originally referred not to its size but to the kind of paint.

The brilliant red color monks used in decorating medieval manuscripts was called minium (red lead) in Latin, and that art was called *miniating*. A picture illuminating the text—necessarily small because of the limited space available—was thus called a *miniature*.

Perfume

A woman's *perfume* derives from Latin *fumus*, "smoke": the smoke or incense arising from a burning sacrifice in ancient religions.

JOB DESCRIPTIONS

Admiral

From the Arabic *amir-al-bahr*, "lord (or king) of the sea."
The *d* may have crept in by association with "admire."*

Assassin

In the 11th and 12th centuries, the *Hashashin* ("hashish eaters") were a secret murder cult of the Ismaili sect of Muslims, followers of the Old Man of the Mountain, Hasan ben Sabah. Originally based at Alamut, south of the Caspian, they spread and became feared throughout Islam.

Marco Polo describes the Old Man offering his followers sensual pleasures, including beautiful maidens, music, and hashish, so that they supposed they were in heaven. He then sent them forth on gangland-style missions to rub out prominent targets, assuring them of a quick trip to paradise if things went sour. (One of the "hashish eaters" stabbed Edward Longshanks at the battle of Acre.)

In 1252 they were broken by the Tatars under Alaü, their fortress leveled, and the Old Man put to death. The *Hashashin* survived in our word *assassin*.

---

* *Admiral King, who led the U.S. Navy in World War II, was thus literally "King of the King," and Columbus, whose Spanish title was "Admiral of the Ocean Sea," becomes "King of the Sea Sea Sea." The title of Admiral returned to Arabic, as described in Ibn Khaldoun's* Prolegomena, *thus becoming a Grand Tour Word: cf. page 56.*

Chauffeur

French for a "heater." Originally this term was used for a particularly nasty breed of robbers, who broke into houses, seized the occupants, and then tortured them by burning their feet in the fireplace until they disclosed where they had stashed their valuables.

Later, the word was applied to stokers of steam engines, including the early automobiles, which ran on steam.

Finally, *chauffeur* came to mean the driver of any car.

Diplomat

Greek for "folded twice." A diplomat dealt in matters so secret that the documents required this special precaution.

Lord

In Old English the head of the house was called the *hlafweard*: "loaf warden," or "master of the bread." This approached the 1960s use of "bread" for "money," or, indeed, the biblical "daily bread."

On the way to *lord* it passed through many intermediate forms, such as *hlaford* and *louerd*.

Similarly, a *lady* was originally the "bread-kneader," *hlaefdige*, before becoming *levedi*, *levdi*, and finally, in the 14th century, *ladi*.

A retainer, in Old English, is a *hlafeta*, "bread-eater."

Pontiff

Pontiff comes from the Latin *pontifex*, "bridge-builder." Once a year in ancient Rome the *pontiffs*, led by their chief, the *pontifex maximus*, or "chief bridge-builder," solemnly threw 23 straw dolls called *argei* into the Tiber. This was to compensate the river-god for the drowned travelers he had forgone as solid bridges replaced leaky rowboats.

With time, the Pope succeeded to the title: in English, Supreme Pontiff. In recent years, however, he has neglected to throw the dolls into the river.

Postman

The term *post* to describe messenger relay stations originated in the 13th century with Marco Polo. He described Kublai Khan's network of more than 10,000 *yambs*, or relay stations, calling them, in Italian, *poste*, or "posts." They were located every 25 to 45 miles on the principal roads throughout the empire. In addition, at 3-mile intervals between the *poste* there were relay stations for runners, who in lieu of the sirens we would use today wore wide belts with bells on them to signal the importance of their business.

Posting in the sense of rising to the motion of a horse's trot also comes ultimately from Marco Polo's expression, as do *postilion*,* *posthaste*, *postage*, and *postman*.

---

* *My favorite expression from a foreign language phrase book is: "Great heavens, the postilion has been struck by lightning."*

PERSONS & PLACES

Arthur

Recent research at Occidental College in California indicates that this quintessentially English hero was actually Artorius, the leader of a Sarmatian band, captured by the Romans under Marcus Aurelius in the steppes of Southern Russia during the second century, A.D. He was reestablished, with his followers, in Northern Britain. The legends they brought with them included tales suggestive of the search for the Holy Grail with similar cup and sword symbolism.

Bistro

From the Russian *bweestra*, "quickly!" It was a favorite command of Russian soldiers in Paris cafés after the fall of Napoleon.

Cambridge

The name of this English university town did not, as one would expect, originally refer to a *bridge* over the *Cam*, which runs through it.

The river's ancient name (by which part of it is still known) was the *Granta*, and the older name for Cambridge was *Grantacester*,* meaning a fortified Roman camp (*castra*) on the Granta.

---

* *Near Cambridge lies the village of Grantchester, celebrated in Rupert Brooke's poems; the name was frozen at that point in its evolution.*

Later it became *Grentbrigseyre*, *Cantbrigge*, and eventually *Cambridge*.

Finally, the river's name was changed, by what is called back-formation, to the *Cam*, to match the name of the town.

Chapel

According to tradition, a 4th century Hungarian soldier, Martin, divided his cloak, or *cappella*, with his sword and gave half of it to a beggar.

After leaving the army he became a professional exorcist, and then retired to a monastery. Thereafter, he was chosen to be bishop of Tours. Eventually he rose to become patron saint of Buenos Aires, as well as of innkeepers and vine-pruners.

The half of his cloak that he had kept became an object of veneration after his death; its shrine or sanctuary thus became known as *cappella* (*Kapelle* in German, *chapelle* in French, *chapel* in English). The custodians of the shrine were for centuries known as *kapellani*.

In a surprising climax to this sequence, when German Jews of the high Middle Ages changed their names to be less conspicuous, families called *Cohen* (priest) often "Germanized" that name into *Kaplan* (chaplain).

Club

Men's hair gathered at the back of the head was once said to be "clubbed," because its shape suggested a cudgel.

Habitual patrons of a coffeehouse sometimes banded together to buy the establishment when its old owner died,

chapel

then installing a new manager and giving it his name: White's Club, Brooks's Club, or whatever. The term *club* was used for this arrangement by analogy to the many strands being brought together in a man's clubbed hair.

Frank

The Franks were a Germanic tribe called by the Romans the *Franci*, after their preferred weapon, the *francus* or javelin. With the erosion of Roman power, the Franks conquered western France down to the Pyrenees. *Franc*, in Old French, came to mean "noble" or "free" (since the Franks had subjugated everyone else) and the word came to imply the virtues of free men: integrity and openness as opposed to the sly obsequiousness of the servile character. A *franklin* was a "freeman" or "freeholder."

In Persian, Arabic, Hindi, and other languages all foreigners are called Franks;* the word also gives us *lingua franca* and *franchise*.

Frankfort, "the ford (river-crossing) of the Franks," gave us the *frankfurter*.

---

* Christian missionaries in Morocco were once called bicouros, meaning "Epicureans." The Moors reasoned that since Europeans were either consuls or traders, and these new arrivals were neither, they must be followers of the heathen philosopher Epicurus, who advised a career of idle pleasure. The missionaries, many of them devoted doctors, were exceedingly vexed by this choice of terms.

Gallery

Literally, "place of the goys." It comes from Italian *galleria*, which comes from Medieval Latin *galeria*, apparently a variant of *galilaea*, the porch of a church (sometimes called in English a *galilee* porch).

Galilaea—or Galilee—in turn comes from the Hebrew *galil hagoyim*: "district of the *goys* (unbelievers)."

Minaret

Nur in Semitic languages means "light." Hebrew *menorah* thus means a "holder of light" or "candelabrum," and Arabic *manarah* means "lighthouse." The Turks used that word for the slender tower next to a mosque, which they felt had features in common with a lighthouse.

PEJORATIVES

Banal

A *ban* once meant a proclaimed order: Indo-European *bha*, "speak." Marriage *banns*, proclaiming a couple's engagement, are still posted on church doors in Catholic countries.

A French *banlieue* or "ban-place," now "suburb," referred to the area controlled by a local authority; where its "writ ran," as lawyers say.

A *moulin à ban* or *four à ban* was a mill or an oven which the lord of the manor provided for his tenants to use in common in return for a share of the output.

The French, and then English, *banal* came from this idea of the common or usual.

Curmudgeon

The origin of this term is a mystery. An anonymous correspondent wrote to Dr. Samuel Johnson suggesting that the word came from *coeur méchant*, French for an "evil heart."

In his great dictionary, Johnson accepted this notion, suggesting that *curmudgeon* derived from "*coeur méchant*, Fr. [meaning *from*] an unknown correspondent."

Then in 1775, *Ash's Dictionary*, in a demented theft from Johnson, announced that *curmudgeon* came "from the French *coeur*, unknown, and *méchant*, a correspondent."

Curmudgeon

Posh

Dunce

The lifelong concern of the great medieval Franciscan theologian *Duns Scotus** was rebutting the theological ideas of the rival order of Dominicans, particularly those of Thomas Aquinas.

Although Duns Scotus succeeded well enough at the time, in later centuries his followers, known as *Dunses*, were counterattacked as dullards and obscurantists.

And with *dunce* the Dominicans seem to have had the last word.

Ostracize

The Greeks wrote names on fragments of broken pottery or tile (*ostrakon*, literally, "oystershell") as ballots when voting to exile someone who represented a danger to the state.

Aristides the Just was once handed a potsherd by an illiterate fellow citizen, who asked him to scratch "Aristides" on it.

As Aristides started to write, he asked the man, "What's so bad about Aristides?"

"I'm just tired of always hearing him called 'the Just,'" the fellow replied.

Posh

The agreeable theory that this word designates the preferred cabin arrangement on the P&O liners to the Far East:

---

* *Properly,* John Duns Scotus; *i.e.,* John *of* Duns *in Berwickshire,* Scotland.

"Port Out, Starboard Home," to avoid the afternoon sun in the Red Sea, cannot be proved. It never occurs in the P&O's records. In the late 19th century it meant, simply, a dandy.

Sycophant

This word, whose modern sense is "flattering parasite; informer," literally means "fig-indicator": Greek *sukon*, "fig," and *phantes*, "one who shows."

The original *sycophants* slyly uncovered dealers in smuggled or stolen figs—a substantial traffic at the time—and then denounced them to the police.

Tawdry

The convent, later cathedral, of Ely was founded in the 7th century by St. Audrey, who died of a growth in her throat, which she believed was a punishment for wearing sumptuous necklaces.

In time, a fair came to be held at Ely on St. Audrey's day, October 17, at which one of the most popular wares was "St. Audrey's lace," a handsome chain or lace band for women to wear around their necks.*

As the centuries passed, the lace was made more and more shoddily, while the saint's name elided into *Tawdry*.†

---

* Lace, *which comes from Latin* laqueus, *"noose," via Old French* las, *originally meant "neck-band."*

† *Just as* St. Clair *has collapsed into* Sinclair.

HIGH FINANCE

Bearish

An ancient proverb in many languages warns against selling a bear skin before you have caught the bear. Thus, for centuries, in English financial jargon stock sold "short"—that is, stock one did not own but sold anyway, hoping to repurchase it cheaper—was known as a "bear skin." The seller was described as a "bear-skin jobber," or "bear": one who stands to profit from a decline in the quotation for a stock; a pessimist.

His opponent, the optimist, has been designated a "bull" at least since the early 18th century.

Capital

From Latin *caput*, a "head" of cattle. Cattle are one of the oldest forms of wealth: they are movable; grow; bear interest (milk); and provide capital gains (calves). Homer valued Ajax's shield in ox hides, and in many cultures a bride-price or damages at law are set in cattle.

Not surprisingly, a number of our financial words derive from this source. *Pecuniary* and *peculation* come from Latin *pecus*, "herd," and *chattel* is cognate with *cattle*.

The Wall Street expression *watered stock* describes cattle who, given salt shortly before reaching a convenient stream, imbibe grossly, increase their weight, and thus fetch an inflated price.

Company

The original sense of *company* survives in our expression, "We're having *company* for dinner"; that is, persons with whom one "breaks bread": Latin *com*, "together," and *panis*, "bread."

The business title & *Co.* adds to company an ampersand: &, which is the last surviving symbol from the oldest known system of shorthand, used in the Roman courts to abbreviate *et*, "and." It is called *ampersand* because centuries ago school recitations of letters began "A *per se* A" and ended "& *per se* And."

Dicker

The Romans used to demand bundles of ten (*decuria*) furs or hides from conquered German tribes as tribute. Over time, the Germans transformed *decuria* into *decura* and later *decher*.

The word reached England and Holland in the Middle Ages as *dyker*. The colonists brought it to America as *dicker* and used it when bartering for furs with the Indians.

From that meaning it evolved into its present sense of "haggle."

Garnish

In business terminology you *garnish* or *garnishee* the salary of someone who owes you money by making his employer turn over part of it to you until the debt is extinguished.

In cooking, to garnish means to "embellish," as by adding a sprig of parsley.

The two words come from the same source, Old French *garnir*, to "prepare," "embellish," or "warn." A fortified town was once called *garnished*, or "prepared." When a warning was issued about the creditworthiness of a person encumbered by debt, he was also said to be *garnished*.

Money

The Romans of the 3rd century B.C., like other people of antiquity, attached their mint to a temple, that of Juno *Moneta*, the "admonisher," from *monere*, "warn." In time, the coins and the mint itself also became known as *moneta*, which is still the Italian word. This gave Spanish *moneda* and French *monnaie*, which then gave English *money*, and Old English *mynet*, "coins," whence English *mint*. *Moidore* comes from Portuguese *moeda de ouro*, "coin of gold."

Dollar comes from *Joachimsthal*, "Joachim's valley" (*thal*) in Bohemia, where in the early 16th century the first *thaler* was minted.

The Spanish dollar, or piece of eight, was the most widely circulated coin in America before the revolution. Our $ sign may be a modified figure 8, to signify that coin, or the initials *U* and *S* superimposed; or a modified £ sign; or, quite possibly, a Phoenician symbol for strength and sovereignty. (There were extensive exchanges between the Phoenicians and the ancient Iberians.) The Spanish believe that the $ sign represents the pillars of Hercules on either side of the Strait of Gibraltar, bound together under Spanish rule.

Philately

This comparatively recent word for the study of postage stamps means literally in Greek, "love of not being taxed," since a stamp meant the letter was carried without further payment.

Similarly, the Modern Greek word for "post office" is *tachydromeion*, "quick-running place" (cf. *Postman*). I particularly like the Modern Greek expression for "national bank": literally, it is an "ethnic trapeze," *ethniki trapeza*. And to pay the bill in a restaurant is to "canonize the logarithm," while a "love affair" is an "erotic hypothesis." A military officer in civvies is said to be wearing "political clothes," from *polis*, "city."

Salary

Salt is indispensable to human life. Foraging animals concentrate salt in their bodies; when we lived as hunters, we got our salt from their flesh. But after we settled down to row-crop agriculture we had to get it artificially, through mining it or boiling or evaporating seawater.

As human settlement spread out from places where salt could be made, more and more it became an object of commerce. All the early caravan tracks across the desert were salt routes, as was the oldest road in Europe, Italy's *Via Salaria*.

The *salarium* was an allowance given to Roman soldiers to buy salt. The word reached us as *salary*.

Tally

Instead of issuing written receipts in financial transactions, from Norman times on the Royal Exchequer cut notches into "tally sticks" (from Latin *talea*, "stick") to indicate amounts of money involved.

The stick, usually about a foot long, but sometimes over six feet, was then split in two. The Exchequer retained one half and gave the other to the second party in the deal. The officials who kept the sticks were called *telliers*, now *tellers*.

In 1834 the authorities resolved to get rid of this hopelessly cumbersome system. The centuries' accumulation of sticks was burned in the furnace of the House of Lords.

The excessive charge of fuel set the building afire. Both Houses of Parliament burned to the ground.

Loo

EQUIPMENT

Ammonia

Ammonia is so called because it was first made from the dung of the worshipers' camels at the temple of Jupiter *Ammon* in Egypt.

Bonfire

A "bone-fire," in which the bodies of the slain were burned after a battle, or a heretic was burned at the stake, or corpses cremated.

Loo

Nobody (except the estimable Thomas Crapper, who perfected the flush toilet) seems eager to accept responsibility for what goes on in the bathroom. Both the French and English words for these matters imply that it all started somewhere else.

Thus, *loo* is considered in England to be a "Frenchy" genteelism, like *demi-tasse*. However, the actual French expression is *lieu à l'Anglaise*, "English place," which throws it right back across the channel.

And one of the most common French words for toilet is *le water*, from the English "water closet."

But the English *toilet* is again a French word, *toilette*, meaning a "little cloth" spread on a lady's bedside table, where the things she might need overnight would be laid out.

Lumber

The Lombards (*Langobardi* in Latin, or "long-beards") were a Germanic tribe who in the 6th century implanted themselves in the Po Valley. Although they were detested there, the area became known as *Lombardy*. Their kingdom was overthrown by the Franks under Charlemagne. Centuries later a number of Lombards spread around Europe as traders and moneylenders. They brought with them the three-ball sign of the pawnbroker, presumably adapted from the arms of the Medici.

London's Lombard Street contained numerous moneylending establishments, essentially pawnshops, which were called *lombards*, pronounced "lumbers."

The rooms where pawned property was stored thus became *lumber* rooms. That term later came to cover storehouses in general, and finally what they sometimes contain: sawn timber.

Pocket-handkerchief

A *poke* (from French *poche*) is a sack, as in the "pig in a poke" that one should think twice about buying. A small *poke* is a *pocket*.

Chef in French is "head" (from Latin *caput*), and a *couvre-chef*, or *kerchief*, is a head-cloth or bandanna. One you keep in hand to sneeze into is a *hand couvre-chef* or *handkerchief*.

So *pocket-handkerchief* means "little-sack-hand-cover-head."

Sarcophagus

Literally, "flesh-eater." The Greeks had a direct way of looking at things.

On the other hand, their word for "cemetery," *koimeterion*, means "sleeping place."

Wig

Wig comes from *periwig*, from the French *perruque*, "wig," which comes from *perroquet*, "parrot," a reference to decorative plumage, just as the English called a dandy a "popinjay."

Perroquet, however, is derived from *Pierrot*, a diminutive of *Pierre*, "Peter."*

That saint, whose attempt to walk on water is described in Matthew 14:29, also gave his name to another bird, the stormy *petrel*, which can live on the waves far out to sea.

Sailors call petrels "Mother Carey's chickens," perhaps by folk-etymology, via a Latin language, from *mater cara*, the "dear mother" Mary.

---

* *Personal names frequently become attached to birds (and animals), e.g.,* jack*daw,* robin *redbreast (originally just redbreast),* mag*pie,* tom*tit,* dickey *bird.*

GAMES

Canter

After the martyrdom and sanctification of Thomas à Becket under Henry II, the saint's grave in Canterbury cathedral became a place of pilgrimage—whence Chaucer's *Canterbury Tales*, told by a group of pilgrims on their way to the shrine.

The gait of their horses became known as the *canterbury*, later the *canter*.

Chess

The object of chess is to trap the *shah*, "king." The winner then announces that the king is "dead" (*mat*): "checkmate," or *shah* mat*.

Shah evolved, through an Old French plural, *esches*, into *chess*; also into *checkers*, both the game and the design.

The *Exchequer*, which in England deals with the financial side of government, probably derived from the checkerboard tables, *eschequier*, used in the Middle Ages to facilitate counting. A bank *check* comes from the same source.

The game of chess seems to have entered Europe with the Arabs, at the time of their conquest of Spain. They had learned it from the Persians, who apparently found it in India.

* *Perhaps also* sheikh.

Hazard

The *hazards* of life once referred to dice. The word comes from Arabic *az-zahr*, "the die." The Crusaders probably brought it back with them to France, whence, as *les hasards*, it crossed to England with the Norman Conquest. Some variants of craps are thus called the *hazards game*.

Ouija

The *ouija* board comes from French *oui* (yes) and German *ja* (yes).

Tennis

Tennis is sometimes said to come from French *tenez*, "hold," a cry supposedly uttered by French players of this ancient Arabic game. But there is no record of such a cry, and the earliest occurrence of even the conjecture is in the 17th century; while *tenetz*, the English adaptation of the original Arabic word, *tanaz*, "leap," goes back to 1400.

Racquet probably comes from Arabic *rahet*, "palm of the hand." The original form of the game was played with the palm alone.

The *c* in racquet doesn't belong there, being a garbling of French *raquette* and English *racket*.

BIRDS & BEASTS

Cab

That modest but determined beast, the goat, prances about our language in many disguises. *Capers* about, one might say. *Capra*, Latin "goat," gives us *caper*, *caprice*, and *capricious*. The leaps of a kid, *cabri* in French, gave *cabriole*, a frisky jump.

In the 18th century *cabriole* meant a light two-wheeled carriage drawn by one horse, doubtless because of its jaunty motion. As *cabriolet*, the vehicle rolled to England, where it shriveled to *cab*.*

Caterpillar

Literally, "hairy cat," from the Old French *chatepelose*.

Gossamer

This word is a contraction of "goose-summer," meaning late October and November.

At that time, the harvest being done, the geese are let into the fields to fatten on the stubble; often on those brilliant days the "gossamer" spider-webs can be perceived hanging among the half-bare branches.

---

* *The English specialize in these brusque contractions. Thus,* mobile vulgus *(fickle crowd) became* mob; sine nobilitate *(without nobility) became* snob; *association football became* soccer; *university,* varsity; *public house,* pub; *zoological garden,* zoo; *and so on.*

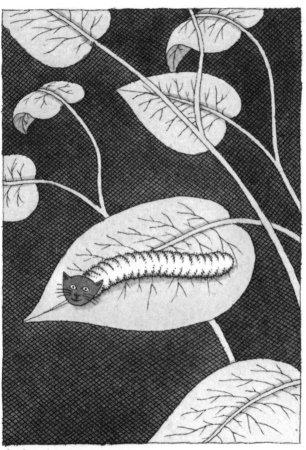

Caterpillar

Tuxedo

Pedigree

Originally, Middle French *pie de grue*, "crane's foot," from a symbol used to indicate lines of descent on genealogical charts.

Tuxedo

Tuxedo in a Delaware Indian dialect means "round foot," a euphemism for "wolf."

It was at Tuxedo Park, New York, that in 1896 Griswald Lorillard cut the tails off his evening coat to create the short dinner jacket, which thus became known as the *tuxedo* . . . in more than one sense, "wolf's clothing."

Ukulele

"Jumping flea" in Hawaiian: *uku*, meaning "flea," and *lele*, meaning "jumping." It was the local nickname for Major Purvis, a retired British officer who popularized the instrument, which had been brought to the islands by Portuguese laborers. Presumably *ukulele* refers to the fingers darting among the strings.

FOOD

Humble Pie

This sinister repast was composed of the *umbles*, or guts, of an animal, and was assigned to the servants, while the gentry enjoyed the steaks and chops.

Ketchup

In the 18th century the Dutch imported this Chinese condiment, originally a spiced mushroom sauce called *ketsiap*, as *ketjap*.

Luncheon

Lunch comes from Scottish *lonch*, a "hunk" of meat.

Nuncheon, an old word for the midday meal, means "noon drink" in Middle English: *nonechenche*.

So *luncheon*, a barbarous combination of the two, makes no sense, meaning, literally, "drinking a hunk of meat."

Marzipan

"Christ enthroned in judgment," *Christos Pantocrator*, was depicted on a Venetian coin. The Saracens were pleased to accept the cash, but not the theology, and so referred to these coins, which circulated widely, as *mauthaban*, "seated king."

Ketchup

Apparently the Venetians exacted the coin, which they came to call *matapanus*, as an import duty.*

In time it came to mean a percentage of a load of produce or merchandise, and eventually to a box that carried that percentage.

Still later it came to mean a similar box containing confections. By folk-etymology the word was then deformed into *Marci panis*, "St. Mark's bread."

In the form of an almond paste candy, it came to England as *marchpane*, the term used there until recently. It then reappeared via Germany as *marzipan*.

Mayonnaise

One of the few surviving words of Carthaginian derivation. Mago, Hannibal's brother, gave his name to Mahon, capital of Minorca. The Duc de Richelieu successfully beseiged it in 1756. During the seige his cook concocted the sauce from eggs and oil, there being no butter or cream on the island, and named it after the town.†

---

* *Our* dime, *similarly, comes from French* dîme, *a tax of a tenth of a load, from Latin* decem, *"ten." Cf.* Dicker, *page 32.*

† *Similarly,* zabaglione *is said to be named after Marshal Baglioni, who defended Florence from Castruccio Castracani in the 15th century. Reduced to eggs and brandy, his cook invented "Baglioni soup,"* zuppa Baglioni, *elided into* zabaglione.

Sirloin

There is no basis to the contention that James I (as suggested by Jonathan Swift), or Henry VIII, Charles II, or any other English king "knighted" a cut of beef, which thus became "Sir Loin," although this myth is found in many popular books of etymology, and has given rise to a mistaken sequel, the *baron* (or double sirloin) of beef.

In reality the word, which was spelled *surloin* until 1600, dates from the 15th century and comes directly from Old French *surlonge*: *sur*—"on" the *longe*—"loin"; in Latin, *super lumbus*.

Tempura

Neither a native Japanese dish, nor, indeed, a Japanese name.

When the Portuguese arrived in the 17th century, the Japanese noticed that at certain "times" (Portuguese, *tempora*) of the year, notably Lent,* they switched from meat to fish. With Oriental subtlety the Japanese concluded that the word for "times" meant a variety of seafood.

* Siesta *also has a religious origin. The monastic day was punctuated by the canonical hours of prayer: matins, prime, nones, vespers, and so on. The "sixth," or* sexta, *evolved into* siesta.

MEDICINE

Delirium

"Out of the furrow" (*lira*) in Latin—referring to a reeling plowman. "Off his trolley," we would say.

Grog

Grog is named after the unpopular Vice Admiral Edward Vernon of the Royal Navy, who fought in the War of Jenkins' Ear. He was a friend of George Washington's brother, whence Mount Vernon.

The Royal Navy customarily doled out a daily tot of rum to the tars, but in 1740 the admiral ordered that water be added to make it harder for them to get drunk. This made him more unpopular than ever.

He was known as "Old Grog" because of his *grogram* cloak (from the French *gros grain*, "rough cloth"), and his nickname stuck to the drink.

Quack

As the bubonic plague, for which there was no cure, decimated Europe, swarms of bogus healers preyed on the desperate populace. Some offered ointments or salves (from Latin *salve*, "save"). Their noisy sales talks, like those of carnival barkers, reminded the Dutch of ducks quacking (*kwakken*). So in Holland they became known as *quacksalvers*, and later *quacks*.

Their Italian confreres, like our soap-box orators, made a practice of mounting the nearest bench (whence *mountebank*, a "charlatan") to extol their own brand of salve or *nostrum* (Latin for "our"). In Italy an epidemic was thought to result from the "influence" (*influenza*, our *flu*) of a malign conjuncture of planets.

℞

In Roman times prescriptions often began with a prayer to Jupiter. Since then they have continued to be written in Latin, but the prayer has shrunk to Jupiter's astrological sign, ℞. Another theory is that ℞ is an abbreviation for the Latin *recipe*, "take."

Venom

The Indo-European *ven* or *wen*, "want" or "desire," led to Latin *venari*, "to hunt," which in turn gave rise to *venison*.

It also brought forth *Venus*, the "venerated" or beloved.

Venice, in turn, took its name from a tribe who called themselves *Veneti*: the "desirables," so to speak, just as the current inhabitants enjoy being called the "beautiful people." From *Venice* came *Venezuela*, "little Venice."

A goblet of *Venice* glass was supposed to break when filled with *venom*,* which originally meant a potion to facilitate lovemaking or *venery*; whence *venereal*, having to do with lovemaking.

---

* *I like Frederick ("Baron Corvo") Rolfe's description of a poisoned glove as a "gauntlet envenomed."*

A herd of elephants

APPENDICES

Terms of Multitude

Every occupation—law, medicine, the sea, agriculture, electronics—has its own precise terminology. Without it, business could not be conducted. That each uses its own set of plurals is, therefore, no surprise. Several vessels for the sailor make a *fleet*, not a *herd*; we have a *library* of books; a *congregation* of worshipers (from Latin *grex*, "flock"); a *portfolio* of securities; and so on.

These words, usually called collective or generic terms or nouns of multitude,* are only surprising to an outsider. The English have always liked to make lists of them, starting with the courtesy (i.e., etiquette) books of the late Middle Ages. Here are the most important ones traditionally used of animals, notably in hunting and hawking. The terms are frequently interchanged.

A *colony* of ants
A *shrewdness* or *troop* of apes
A *pace* of asses
A *cete* of badgers
A *shoal* of bass
A *sloth* of bears
A *colony* of beaver†
A *swarm* of bees
A *singular* of boars (cf. page 58.)
A *clouder* of cats (often corrupted into *clowder*; perhaps originally *cluster*)
An *army* of caterpillars

A *drove* of cattle
A *brood* of chickens (but a *clutch* of eggs)
A *rag* of colts
A *murder* of crows
A *cowardice* of curs
A *dole* (formerly *dule*) or *piteousness* of doves or turtledoves
A *paddling* of duck (swimming)
A *raft* of duck (collected in the water, e.g., to sleep)
A *team* of duck (in flight)

---

* *They are* terms of venery *only if they relate to hunting (Latin* venari*); and are never* venereal, *whose only meaning is "sexual." Cf. page 51.*

† *The final* s *is often omitted when an animal is thought of as game.*

A *herd* of elephants

A *gang* of elk

A *business* of ferrets or flies*

A *charm* of finches

A *school* of fish

A *skulk* or *troop* (and sometimes *cloud* or *earth*) of foxes (which, however, are solitary animals)

A *gaggle* of geese (stationary)

A *skein* of geese (flying)

A *trip* of goats

A *cluster* of grasshoppers

A *cast* of hawks (two)

A *brood* of hens

A *siege* of herons

A *drift* of hogs

A *harras* of (stud) horses (still used in Latin languages)

A *pack* of hounds

A *swarm* of insects

A *troop* of kangaroos

A *kindle* or *litter* of kittens

A *deceit* of lapwings

An *exaltation*, *ascension*, or *bevy* of larks

A *leap* of leopards

A *pride* of lions

A *plague* or *swarm* of locusts

A *tidings* of magpies

A *stud* (sic) of mares

A *richness* of martens

A *nest* of mice

A *troop* or *shrewdness* of monkeys

A *barren* of mules (perhaps originally *bearing* or *burden*)

A *watch* of nightingales

A *parliament* of owls

A *covey* of quail

A *muster* or *ostentation* of peacocks

A *nye* or *covey* of pheasants (on the ground)

A *bouquet* of pheasants (rising)

A *congregation* of plovers

A *string* of ponies

A *litter* of pups

A *nest* of rabbits

An *unkindness* of ravens

A *crash* of rhinoceroses

A *bevy* of roebucks

A *pod* of seal (or *harem* of females)

---

* *A* freamyng *of ferrets occurs in Sladen's* The Complete Crossword Reference Book, *London, 1949, in a list of collective nouns, along with* pride *of lions and so on. It is found nowhere else. Nuttall's* Standard Dictionary, *Fifth Edition, London, 1932–50, has* fesning, *from which Sladen copied it incorrectly. Nuttall, in turn, miscopied it from* fesymes *in Beard's* American Boys' Book of Wild Animals, *Philadelphia, 1921. This is apparently an error for* fesynes, *which occurs in Strutt's* The Sports and Pastimes of the People of England, *London, 1838. That, in turn, is a misprint for* besynes (i.e., business) *of ferrets, which occurs in the 15th century* Book of Saint Albans.

A *flock* of sheep
A *bed* of snakes
A *wisp* or *walk* of snipe
A *host* of sparrows
A *dray* of squirrels
A *murmuration* of sandpipers
 or starlings
A *sounder* of swine
A *spring* of teal

A *knot* of toads
A *rafter of turkeys*
A *bale* of turtles
A *nest* of vipers or wasps
A *pod* or *gam* of whales
A *pack* or *route* of wolves
A *fall* of woodcock
A *descent* of woodpeckers

Rhyming Slang

We often don't realize how many American expressions are Cockney rhyming slang. The principle is illustrated by calling a girl a "twist and twirl" (usually shortened to "twist"), or a wife, "trouble and strife," and so on. Thus "facts" in Cockney became *brass tacks*, as in our "let's get down to brass tacks."

"Beer" became *pig's ear*.

La-de-dah refers to someone fancy enough to own a "car" (pronounced cah).

"Eat" became *Dutch treat*, from "Dutch Street," where there were a number of eating places.

"No hope" became *no soap*.

"Fart" became *raspberry tart*, as in "Give 'em the *raspberry*," or *razz*.

"Go" became *scapa flow* or *scapa*. This English expression (pronounced scah-pa) overlaps *scarper* (Parlyaree—circus language— meaning to desert a play or quit one's lodgings without paying). *Scarper* comes from the Italian *scappare* "escape," from the Latin *excappa*, to slip "out of one's cape" when arrested. *Scarper* has another sense, soft footwear (in which to escape the police), presumably influenced by Italian *scarpa*, "shoe."

Grand Tour Words

Words sometimes set forth from one country and after sojourns abroad reappear quite changed. I have never seen a list of such "round trip" expressions, so they are hard to collect; one just has to be alert as one goes along.

French *boeuf*, "beef," for example, sallied forth to England with the Normans, was accepted as *beefsteak*, and recently returned to the Académie Française dictionary as *biftek*.

Some women may be aware that what we call a *redingote* is the French word for our *riding coat*, having come back around a circular course. Few citizens of Genoa, however, know that their blue *jeans* are named after the English pronunciation of the French name, *Gênes*, for their own city. Nor are the burghers of Nîmes conscious that the *denim* their jeans are made from came centuries ago from Nîmes itself (*de Nîmes*). Still another fabric, *mohair*, or goat's wool cloth, emigrated to France as *moiré*, and was reintegrated into English as *moire*, or watered silk.

Many words have been altered by a sojourn south of the border. For example, a Frenchman speaking of *mariachi* music is referring to *les mariages*, at which it was played when the French occupied Mexico. A *freebooter* is a highwayman or land pirate. In Central America he became known as a *filibustero*. The word returned to America as *filibuster*, and acquired its new sense of a drawn-out oration.

Travelers to India who stay in a *bungalow* are often unaware that the English word started out there as *Bangalore*.

Un coctel, from our "cocktail," is now good French; it may derive from American Creole *cocktay*, from French *coquetier*, the "egg-cup" in which it was served.

For *grog*, see page 50.

The young man who today accompanies a Frenchman playing golf, was in his earlier days a *cadet*, "youth," who made his way to Scotland, was rechristened a *caddie*, and then returned to the golf courses of France as *le caddie*.

For *flirt* see page 16.

Many Grand Tour words are the labels put by Portuguese explorers to what they found in their travels, which later returned to Europe as authentic native imports.

Caste is Portuguese *casta*, "chaste" or "pure."

Cobra is from the Portuguese word for "snake."

Fetish is Portuguese *feitiço*, from the Latin *facticius*, a "made thing."

A *joss* stick is Portuguese *deos*, from the Latin *deus*,* "god."

Corral is Portuguese *curral*, from the Dutch *kraal*.

Mandarin is Portuguese *mandarim*, from a Malay word meaning an "official."

Palaver is Portuguese *palavra*, "word."

Tank is Portuguese *tanque*, a "pool" or "cistern."

For *tempura*, see page 49.

Redundancies

Throughout history many redundancies, or pleonasms, arose when new arrivals questioned local inhabitants about names for things.

Thus, Torpenow Hill, near Plymouth, England, means "hill hill hill hill": Saxon *tor*, Celtic *pen*, Scandinavian *how* and Middle English *hill*.

        Act I
Saxon invader: What do you call that *tor*?
Celt: A *pen*, of course.
Saxon invader: Right, we'll call it Tor Pen.

        Act II
Viking invader: You! What's that *how* called?
Saxon descendant: Torpen.
Viking: Okay, from now on it's Torpen How.

---

* Dyaus, *the Sanskrit word for "day" and "heaven," is in turn the source of* Zeus, deus, Jupiter *(day-father), and* Tiu, *son of Odin in Nordic myth, and the god of war.* Tiu, *in turn, gave us* Tuesday, *which corresponds to French* mardi, *"Tuesday," from Latin* Mars, *also the god of war.*

Act III

Middle Englishman: I say, what do you call that hill over there?

Viking descendant: Well, sir, we folks hereabouts calls it Torpenow, we does.

Middle Englishman: Indeed! Well, as you like. Torpenow Hill it is.

Similarly, when Captain Cook asked the name of an Australian marsupial, the natives answered *kangaroo,* meaning "I don't know." And the French word for "transom" is *vasistas*—German for "What's that?"

For *Admiral of the Ocean Sea* cf. footnote, page 18.

A *cheerful countenance* means a "faceful face." *Cheer*, Middle English "face," comes from the French *chère*, "face," as in *faire bonne chère*, "be of good cheer."

A *demitasse cup* is a "half cup cup."

Disheveled hair means "unhaired hair."

Dry Sack means "dry dry." *Sack* comes from French *sec*, "dry"; whence German *Sekt*, champagne.

Marline line is "tying line line."

A *mess mate* is a "food food": French *mets*, "food," plus a variation of "meat."

A *pea jacket* is a "jacket jacket," from the Dutch *pij*, a sailor's garment.

Prosciutto ham is "ham ham."

Reindeer comes from Old Norse *hreinn*, "reindeer," and *dyr*, "deer."

The Sahara Desert is "desert desert."

A *saltcellar* comes from the French *salière*, salt dispenser, and so means "salt salter."

Shrimps scampi are "shrimps shrimps."

A *singular of boars* (cf. Terms of Multitude) comes from the French *sanglier*, "boar," and is thus a "boar of boars."

Reduplications

Fiddle-faddle: Fiddle is a corruption of *Vitula*, the Roman goddess of victory and jubilation, which are often accompanied by music.

Hobson-jobson: On the holy day of Ashura the faithful cry out, *"Ya Hasan, Ya Husein,"* to mourn the murder of the two grandsons of Mohammed. British army slang turned this into *hobson-jobson*, which sounded more reasonable, meaning a hubbub or tumult. Any folk-etymology is thus called a *hobson-jobson*.

Hocus-pocus: From *hic est corpus*, "this is the body" in the Roman mass. *Hoax* is a contraction of *hocus*. (*Patter*, meaning a "rapid-fire spiel," comes from the Latin name for the Lord's Prayer, *Pater noster*, "Our Father.")

Hugger-mugger: This term for mysterious skulduggery is a variation of *hoker-moker*, from Middle English *mokeren*, "conceal."

Hurly-burly: This 16th-century expression for "uproar" evolved from *hurling* (fighting) *and burling*, a 15th-century jingle. There is presumably a connection with *hurluberlu*, which occurs in Rabelais, and Greek *hurliburli*, "headlong." One thinks with satisfaction of Mrs. Pat Campbell's description of marriage as a transfer from "the hurly-burly of the chaise longue to the decorum of the double bed."

Mumbo jumbo: Originally a tribal god, priest, or fetish of the Mandingos of the western Sudan. The name apparently derives from *Mama*, a "grandmother" or "ancestor," and *dyambo*, "headdress" (or perhaps *gyo*, "trouble," and *mbo*, "leave").

Nitty-gritty: Originally, black slang for the inner end of the vagina.

Surprising Family Names

Adam(s) Percy: Hebrew, "red."*

Algernon: Moustached. A particular given name of the Spencer family, applied at a time when moustaches were unusual.

Atterbury: At the fort. *Ter* is the obsolete feminine dative singular of "the."

Blood: From Welsh *Ap-Lud*, "Son of Lud" or "Ludwig."

Brock: Badger.

Calvert: Calfherd.

Cameron: Gaelic, "hook-nose."

Cass: Diminutive of *Cassandra*, a feminine form of *Alexander*.

Cecil: From Latin *caecus*, "blind." *Sheila* is from the same source via *Cecilia*.

Cheever: Old French, "she-goat."

Coffin: French *chauvin*, "bald."

Coward: Cowherd.

Denis(e): Follower of Dionysius.

Devereux: French "from Évreux," which took its name from the Celtic tribe known as the Eburuci because they lived on the River Ebura (or Eure), which, in turn, comes from the word for "yew tree" in Gaulish.

Fitch: Polecat.

---

* *There were plenty of red-haired or red-skinned people in Britain at the time surnames were assigned, but the color is almost always camouflaged, as Reid, Rudd, Rowse, Rous, Rouse, Rose, Russell, Rufus, Gough, or some other variant.*

Hollister: A female brothel-keeper* or madam (in the masculine, *Hollyer*).

Kellogg: Kill-hog; a hog butcher.

Kennedy: "Hideous head" in Irish.

Lazar: "Leper," Lazarus.

MacArthur: Son of Arthur; but see page 21.

Popper: On an envelope, *Frankfort* can be abbreviated *FF*; in Hebrew, which has no separate capital *F*, this is written *PP*. Over time, persons who lived in *PP* were eventually called *Popper*.

Powell: Welsh *Ap-Howell*, "son of Howell," just as *Pugh* comes from *Ap-Hugh*.

Purcell: French *pourcel*, "little pig."

Seward: Sowherd.

Walker: Not, as one might suppose, the guardian of a village (who was the *ward*); rather, the man who trampled the cloth being bleached in the vat of the *fuller*.

---

* *Many English occupation names add an "s" to give the feminine form: e.g., Baker-Baxter; Spinner-Spinster; Webber-Webster.*

INDEX